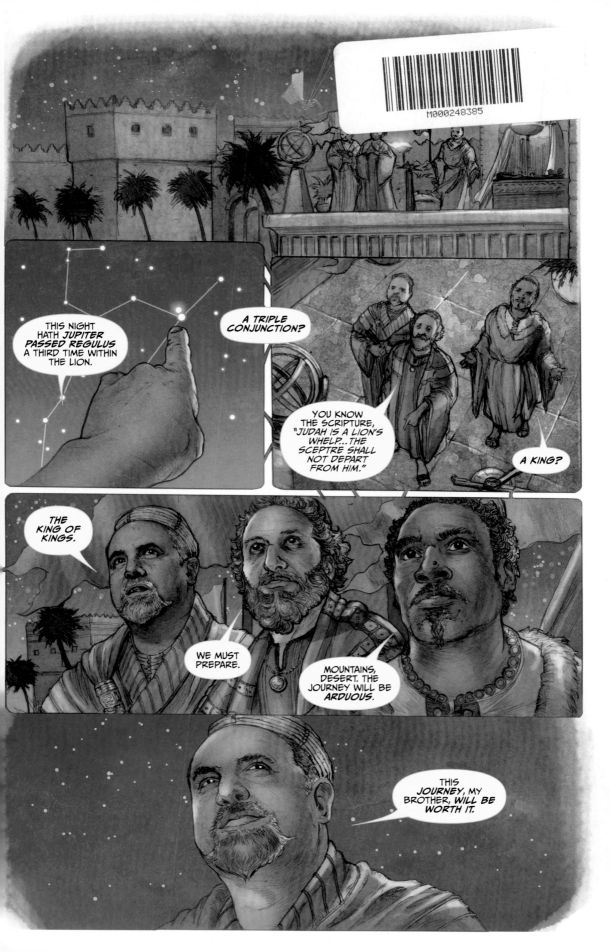

Apostle Arts Presents...

ACHILL

Based on the Gospels Ac
By Billy Tucci with
Bill Tortolini – Letters, Barry Orki
Edited b
Cover by Billy Tu
With Special Thanks to Rick La

DisBORN

...ling to Matthew and Luke

...ors by Paul Mounts

...Design, Mike Renzine – Production

... Vaughn

...nd Mark Sparacio

..., Evan Archilla, and Jason Peet

Apostle Arts, LLC.

BUT HOW CAN THIS BE, SEEING NO MAN HAS EVER TOUCHED ME?

THOU HAST FOUND FAVOR WITH *GOD*.

YOUR CHILD WILL BE GREAT, AND TAKE THE THRONE OF DAVID.

AND HE SHALL REIGN OVER THE HOUSE OF JACOB FOREVER.

FOR HE IS *THE SON OF GOD* AND HIS KINGDOM SHALL HAVE NO END.

BUT THERE IS MORE *GOOD NEWS*.

THY COUSIN ELIZABETH IS WITH *CHILD!* EVEN IN OLD AGE AND PRESUMED BARREN, SHE IS NOW IN HER SIXTH MONTH OF PREGNANCY.

FOR WITH GOD, *NOTHING IS IMPOSSIBLE.*

THEN LET ALL THAT YOU SAY FOR ME COME TRUE...

FOR I AM THE SERVANT OF THE LORD.

And it came to pass that the Emperor Caesar Augustus decreed that all subjects of Rome return to the lands of their ancestors and be taxed.

"GOD IS WITH US."

So Mary accompanied her husband, a descendant of King David, from the town of Nazareth to Joseph's ancestral home of **Bethlehem** to register for the census.

And it was there, in the lowliest of places, that Mary brought forth a **son**, swaddled him in strips of cloth and laid him in a manger.

And bowed before the Miracle of Christmas.

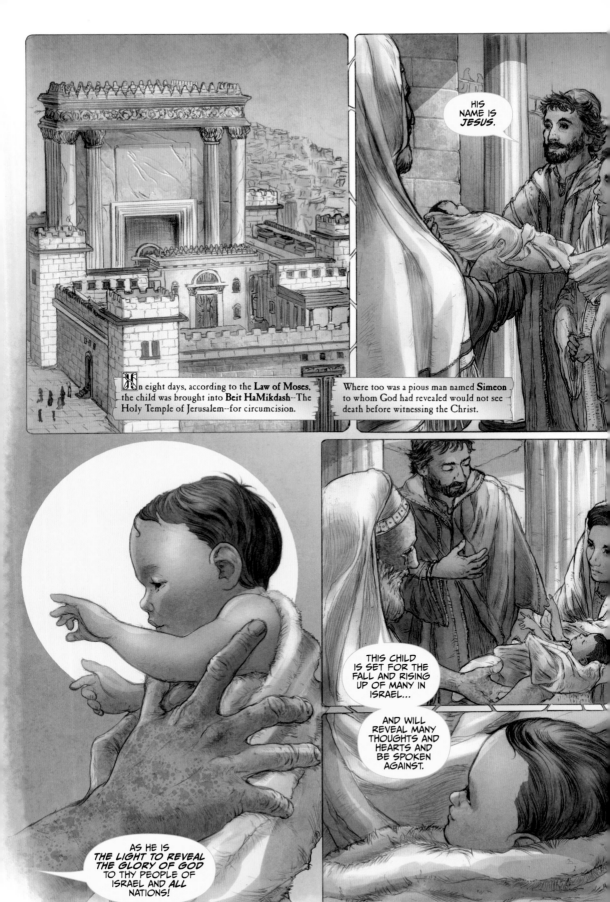

On eight days, according to the **Law of Moses**, the child was brought into **Beit HaMikdash**--The Holy Temple of Jerusalem--for circumcision.

Where too was a pious man named **Simeon** to whom God had revealed would not see death before witnessing the Christ.

HIS NAME IS *JESUS.*

THIS CHILD IS SET FOR THE FALL AND RISING UP OF MANY IN ISRAEL...

AND WILL REVEAL MANY THOUGHTS AND HEARTS AND BE SPOKEN AGAINST.

AS HE IS *THE LIGHT TO REVEAL THE GLORY OF GOD* TO THY PEOPLE OF *ISRAEL* AND *ALL* NATIONS!

GOD BLESS US! NOW YOUR SERVANT MAY DIE IN PEACE AS YOU PROMISED...

FOR MY EYES HAVE SEEN THE *SAVIOR*, WHOM YOU HAVE PREPARED FOR ALL...

HOSHANA!

FOR A SWORD SHALL PIERCE YOUR VERY SOUL.

BUT PRAISE GOD, YOUR SERVANT, *ANNA*, WILL EXCLAIM TO ALL WHO HAVE WAITED FOR JERUSALEM'S REDEMPTION... YOUR SON HAS COME!

FOR OVER SIXTY YEARS, I HAVE LIVED A WIDOW'S LIFE DAY AND NIGHT WITHIN THESE TEMPLE WALLS.

MANY MONTHS AGO, THE LIGHTS OF JUPITER AND VENUS JOINED TOGETHER IN THE MOST BRILLIANT DISPLAY WE'D EVER SEEN. WE FOLLOWED THE FIRST HERE TO JERUSALEM.

THEN GO UNTO BETHLEHEM AND SEARCH HIGH AND LOW FOR THIS CHILD...

AND WHEN YOU'VE FOUND HIM, SEND WORD TO THE PALACE SO THAT I, TOO, MAY COME AND WORSHIP HIM.

hen they departed from Herod the star went before them, till it came and stood over where the young child was...

BROTHERS-- LOOK!

PRAISE HEAVEN! WHAT PLACE IS MORE FITTING FOR THE CHILD OF GOD THAN THE MOST HUMBLE OF HOMES?

And when they came into the house, they saw the young child with Mary his mother, and fell down and worshipped him.

And opened their treasures and presented unto him these gifts...

GOLD.

FOR THE KING OF KINGS.

FRANKINCENSE.

FOR THE MOST DIVINE AND HIGHEST OF PRIESTS.

MYRRH...

FOR HIS *ULTIMATE SACRIFICE* FOR THE SINS OF MAN.

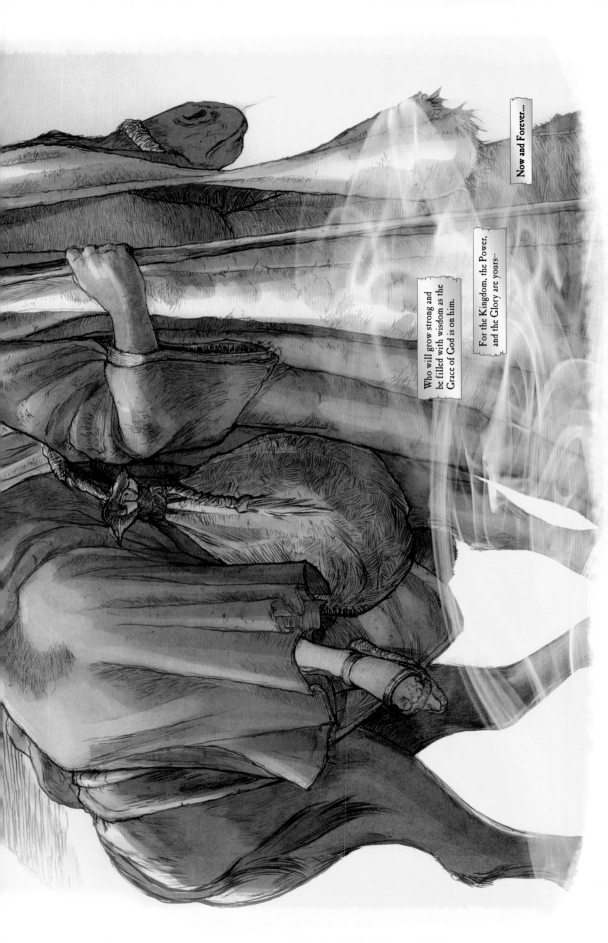

"The heavens declare the glory of God; the skies proclaim the work of his hands. Day after day they pour forth speech; night after night they reveal knowledge."

— Psalm 19:1-2 (NIV)

The Star of Bethlehem fascinates. For millennia, believers, scoffers, and the curious have wondered at the Biblical account of the Star. The Bible recounts unusual, or even impossible astronomical events at Christ's birth. But what happens if we combine current historical scholarship, astronomical fact, and an open mind?

I first asked this question over a decade ago. A lawyer by trade, I became fascinated—obsessed, really—with figuring out the Star. Sitting in the dark on my back deck, my eyes to the heavens and my laptop crunching numbers in an astronomical software program, I uncovered a celestial poem so beautifully written it changed my life forever.

And I am not alone.

Fast forward to summer, 2011, and the day Billy Tucci had a friend ring me about contributing to a graphic novella interpretation of the Christmas story. At first, I wasn't sure what to make of it. What I was unaware of at the time—and something Billy's fans have known for years—is that Billy is obsessed with *details*. Every line Billy's pencil carves is informed by meticulous research. He's not above dressing his friends in period costume and posing them in still-life reenactments if it will improve the page. Some people think Billy goes overboard on this detail stuff. I don't, because I'm the same way. (I'm a lawyer, remember?)

And that's why, when Billy's friend called, my mobile phone danced in my pocket. You see, Billy being Billy wanted the Star in this book to be spot-on accurate. Many people don't realize that the neighborhood nativity scenes get it wrong. The Magi weren't manger-side the night of Jesus' birth; they arrived months later, guided by something visible to all but that only a few could really see. Billy knew from my DVD, *The Star of Bethlehem*, that I'd seen the Star. Maybe I could help him—and you—see it too.

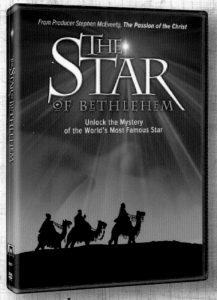

The science behind the Star begins with a five-hundred-year-old Austrian brainstorm that's still shocking and sizzling today. Back then, Johannes Kepler puzzled out his three Laws of Planetary Motion. Kepler's conclusion? The universe and our solar system run smoothly, like a great mathematical clock. Centuries later, NASA (and everyone else) uses Kepler's laws to calculate paths for space probes. Think about it—spacecraft slingshot through a black vacuum at unreal speeds for decades and arrive at precisely the correct bit of space and time to do their work.

Learn more at
www.bethlehemstar.net

But Kepler's math also works in reverse. Running Kepler's stopwatch backward allowed me to show scientifically that Christ's Star wasn't some goofy invention of early believers trying to embellish Jesus' birth. *The Star was a real astronomical event.* An event strongly supported by 1) Kepler's math (in the form of computer software), and 2) every clue I could pry out of the Bible, including the original Greek texts. In fact, if you take the time, you can find nine specific clues about the Star in Matthew's original gospel account. It's those nine clues that drove my pursuit of the Star. And it's the evidence they illuminate that brought Billy Tucci and me together in this book.

So, what happens when you combine current historical scholarship, astronomical fact, and an open mind? I invite you to visit *www.bethlehemstar.net* and join the tens of millions of people worldwide who discovered for themselves the truth about history's most famous star. If you'd like to hear me tell the story and show you what the Magi saw 2,000 years ago, pick up a copy of my DVD, *The Star of Bethlehem*—a fun and fascinating presentation that's also one of the best-selling indie documentaries on Earth.

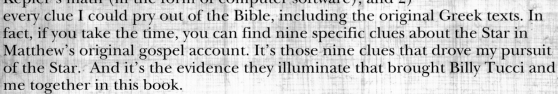

God bless and go for broke, Billy!

Rick Larson
The Star of Bethlehem

The Road to Bethlehem

"Dad, why do you want to do the birth of Jesus instead of a super-hero book?"

My eldest son's query wasn't the first time I'd been asked that question. Perhaps some of you are also wondering why, in a genre dominated by cowls and capes, would anyone do a comic book on the Christmas story?

I have been very blessed in life to continually support my family by doing what I love for a living: writing, illustrating, and publishing comic books. It's been a very colorful and rewarding career, but there has been one project that's always eluded me, that *dream* project for which every artist longs. Now, thanks to some wonderful friends and family, that dream has come true for me.

The story of Christmas holds such importance to so many people on so many levels that taking it on was definitely the most intimidating professional decision of my life. After all, how arrogant can someone be to believe that he's the one to tell *this* story? I guess it all comes down to faith, really. I am a "Christian" who, *finally*, after years of hearing it, answered the call to share the most beautiful story ever told. I hope I have succeeded and that my love for *A Child Is Born* shows on every page.

And what a story it is! One that is filled with heartbreak, joy, danger, fear, awe, love, and hope all compacted into just a few short New Testament verses! What a challenge it is to follow the Gospels of Matthew and Luke faithfully, while trying to fill in many of the blanks in-between. God's words were the star that guided our ship through this amazing journey, but he had two earthly pilots to read them: my partners — my *brothers* — Evan Archilla and Dr. Jason Peet. It was Evan and Jason and their families who took the greatest leaps of faith (perhaps spiritually, definitely financially) in trusting me with this cherished story. Guys, you are Apostle Arts and I am forever indebted to your generosity and friendship.

Our initial fellowship was soon joined by editor J.C. Vaughn — whose faith is as strong as his encouragement — as well as an amazing cast of artisans: the extraordinary Paul Mounts, who made every panel a painting, Bill Tortolini, the master of letters, cover painter Mark Sparacio, and designers Barry Orkin and Mike Renzine. Words can never express my most sincere gratitude for all that you've done; please know in my heart that I will never, ever forget your feats.

Good News Like This is Meant to be Shared!

Billy Tucci's *A Child is Born* is available for bulk purchase. Give the books away, resell them, or use them as a fundraiser.*

Visit www.achildisbornbook.com/bulksales for more details.

*Be sure to check with your tax advisor.

I must also thank all my friends who helped by posing for me bearing hockey sticks and stuffed dinosaurs (in place of staffs and lambs) in my attempts to recreate that far off world still impacting history today.

Additionally, a special "thank you" is due to the wonderful Mr. Rick Larson for opening my eyes to the constellations through his personal pursuit of the Star of Bethlehem. You have inspired us all to never look at Jupiter the same way again.

Again, thank you all for giving me a gift that has become the highlight of my career — and one unforgettable and joyous adventure. From now on, we are all brothers in arts!

When I first started researching the book, I met with the Rev. Fr. John from St. John's Greek Orthodox Church. He was very generous with his time, answering my questions and lending me many books and DVDs from various Nativity scholars. One thing he said that really struck me after our first meeting was his admonition not to "lose your faith over this." What Fr. John meant was the more research I did trying to tie all the ends together, the more questions I might raise. Once I started this journey, though, I was never alone. It's been quite epic, really, regarding the many challenges and failures I've come up against. But for every fall there was always someone to raise me up, to befriend me, to encourage me as they too came along on the road to Bethlehem. Because of *A Child Is Born*, I've seen, felt, and learned so much…and my faith has never been stronger.

In closing, I cannot forget my beautiful wife, Deborah, and her great victory over breast cancer this past year. It was your fight, Honey, which steered me down "the right path" career-wise. You made me realize how wonderful life, love, and family truly are; that, at this point in our lives, no work is more worthwhile to our family than illustrating this story of Mary and Joseph.

So how did I answer my son's innocent question on why *A Child Is Born?* It was actually quite simple, "Jesus *is* a super-hero, William — the greatest super-hero ever to walk the earth!"

Thanks be to God!
Billy Tucci

Billy's original graphite illustration of the Virgin and Child. This image serves as the cover artwork to the

A Child Is Born - Artist's Edition.